PRUNED & PREJUDICED

And Other Novel Verses

Based on Jane Austen's

EMMA
SENSE AND SENSIBILITY
NORTHANGER ABBEY
PERSUASION
MANSFIELD PARK
and
PRIDE AND PREJUDICE

Verses by Margaret Dews
Illustrated by J. Christine Fitton

Published by Jeremy Mills Publishing Limited

Published by Jeremy Mills Publishing Limited for the
Northern Branch of the Jane Austen Society.

ISBN 978–1–905217–27–4

For sales and distribution enquiries please visit:
www.jeremymillspublishing.co.uk
or
www.janeaustensociety.org.uk
(Northern Branch page)

CONTENTS

In memory of

Gill Tait

for her enthusiasm and encouragement
during the writing of these verses

Essential Emma

THE WHITE HART INN
Come take the path
That leads to BATH
For a healthy life
and a handsome wife!
MARRIED
Miss Smith
HIGHBURY DATING AGENCY
Prop. Miss E. Woodhouse
SCHOOL
Wealthy
Clergy
RICH
and young
MARRIED
YOUR FACE COULD BE HERE
Self made
Farmer
HIM
1 Money
2 Rank
3 Charm
4 Looks
5 Age
HER
1 Beauty
2 Youth
3 Charm
4 Rank
5 Money

Miss Emma Woodhouse, it was said, was handsome, clever, rich, well bred,
The shining star (with her papa) of Highbury society.
Her sister and her governess had both left home to wed, no less:
A happy state, though Emma's pater viewed it with anxiety.

Her governess and friend for life was now dear Mr Weston's wife.
Frank was his son, an absent one – the mystery was exquisite!
Miss Bates's niece had met the man in Weymouth, so the rumour ran;
The rest just waited for the date he'd deign to come and visit.

Now Emma had a certain skill: it gave her just the greatest thrill
To find a 'catch', the perfect match for some unwitting local.
The Reverend Elton had no mate – he seemed the ideal candidate.
Her neighbour, Mr Knightley, though, was rightly very vocal:

Her meddling was *not* the way! But Emma had a protégée,
A pretty lass who had no class and could have been much brighter.
A worthy farmer was her beau – not Emma's choice: he had to go!
To marry little Harriet to Elton would delight her.

So Emma did what was required, but all too soon the plot misfired
And Harriet, Miss Smith, forthwith was sadly disabused.
In the confines of a carriage Elton offered *Emma* marriage
With a fervour to unnerve her. Well, of course, the girl refused.

The man was of a lower rank – and anyway she fancied Frank!
Dear Mrs Weston's stepson fired her wild imagination.
So Elton took himself to Bath, and there Miss Hawkins crossed his path...
They planned to wed. The news soon spread and caused a mild sensation.

Let's leave this happy pair in peace and contemplate Miss Bates's niece:
Reserved and cool, she was no fool; and though not pert or pretty
Jane Fairfax, when she sang and played, put poor dear Emma in the shade.
They did not hit it off one bit, which really was a pity.

Frank Churchill (his adoptive name) was due at last; and when he came
He charmed his pa and new mama. He charmed Miss Woodhouse too.
But then to London town he sped – to have his hair cut, it was said,
Which Mr Knightley rightly deemed a silly thing to do.

Soon after this a piano came – an unexpected gift for Jane.
But who had sent the instrument? Her guardian? Or a lover?
"George Knightley!" Mrs Weston guessed. Our Emma, though, was unimpressed;
She'd not agree that he could be attached to any other.

Then Frank went home and Emma cooled; he'd flirted but she wasn't fooled,
Nor was she fraught – in fact she thought that *Harriet* might gain.
She never in a million years thought Frank might have his own ideas,
But in the post, unknown to most, sweet letters came for Jane.

Now Frank came back – the Eltons too; the wife was vulgar through and through.
Pushy and vain, she warmed to Jane; kept Emma at a distance.
Elton himself before them all snubbed Harriet at Highbury's ball,
But sprightly Mr Knightley gave Miss Smith his kind assistance.

Next day she suffered yet more pain, attacked by gypsies in the lane.
This time 'twas Frank she had to thank; he calmed the girl's hysteria.
Her heart was filled with gratitude. She fell into romantic mood...
Great was the debt. She loved – and yet the man was so superior.

POST
OFFICE
MISS J.
FAIRFAX

Then came a picnic on Box Hill, and all was going well until
A joke from Emma poking fun at dear Miss Bates's chatter
Upset the poor defenceless soul. George Knightley found it far from droll!
Emma, he claimed, should be ashamed: it was no laughing matter.

His criticism hit her hard; she felt she'd lost his high regard.
Her silly pride was mortified; with anguish she was riven.
So, humbled and without delay, she visited Miss Bates next day.
It was a start. It touched his heart – and Emma was forgiven.

Contrition brought its due reward: their perfect amity restored.
Frank Churchill then made news again – he had a secret lover!
Since Weymouth he had been engaged; a great deception had been staged.
He loved dear Jane – the truth now plain. Would Harriet recover?

Well, yes – because it was not he who'd touched her heart so tenderly,
But Knightley, she said brightly. Emma's soul was filled with terror...
It dawned at last that she alone must have George Knightley for her own,
That all along she'd got it wrong: a devastating error!

He came to bring her sweet relief, believing Frank had caused her grief;
She put him right – what sweet delight! Their hearts both felt the tremor...
Then Frank wrote to apologise; the piano had been *his* surprise.
He made amends and all were friends – including Jane and Emma.

Now Harriet could wed her beau and Emma could wed George, although
This news first met with some regret and fatherly dejection.
So, choosing not to move too far, they started married life with pa –
To his delight: he gained at night a son-in-law's protection.

....so very obliging!

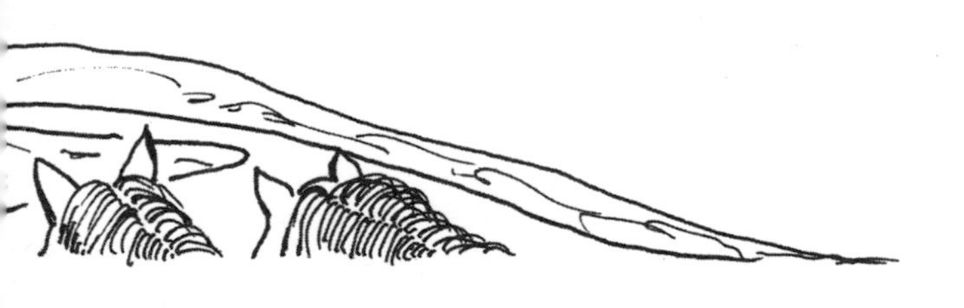

Nonsense

&

Sensibility

GOLD
GOLD
GOLD
THINK of your SON!
They don't need much!
I need a greenhouse!
You need to buy another farm!
You really should enclose the common
She has got all the crockery.
I want a flower garden...
WILL! WILL! MAY! COULD!
SHOULD! WOULD....
LESS – EVEN LESS..
WON'T
PERHAPS...
LATER..
HENRY DASHWOOD
Last WILL
and testament... LOOK AFTER MY WIFE AND DAUGHTERS

When Mr Henry Dashwood died, his wife and daughters were denied
Their legacy; quite honestly his son and spouse were greedy.
By John and Fanny dispossessed, the ladies left their Sussex nest
And moved from here to Devonshire, distressed and rather needy.

The eldest daughter, Elinor, coped well but suffered all the more
Because she'd gone and left the one whose heart she'd seemed to capture.
Her younger sister, Marianne, found Edward nice, but as a man
Too mild and tame, which was a shame – *she* looked for fire and rapture!

At Barton new friends filled their life: Sir John, their cousin, and his wife.
His ma-in-law was thrilled – she saw the girls as wedding fodder:
Dear Colonel Brandon was just right! He fell for Marianne at sight;
She thought him old (he felt the cold!) and something of a plodder.

Now Marianne loved nature's power, but one day in a heavy shower
She slipped and fell – the pain was hell! By chance a passing stranger
Saw both her anguish and her charms and swept her up into his arms
Then onward strode, his precious load soon home and out of danger.

John Willoughby (the stranger's name) was smitten – every day he came;
They shared fond looks and talked of books and music with a passion.
Soon Mrs Dashwood saw a match, for Willoughby seemed quite a catch,
And Brandon was abandoned in a rather careless fashion.

Then Willoughby called round to say he must to London straight away;
He'd be long gone. Well, thereupon poor Marianne was broken:
Exhaustion came from lack of sleep and memories just made her weep;
Her grief grew worse as she'd rehearse the tender words they'd spoken.

At least, though, Elinor could smile, for Edward came and stayed a while.
There on his finger was a ring and she with some elation
Saw that it held her plaited hair. Would Edward Ferrars now declare
His feelings? No – when time to go there'd been no affirmation.

Bemused, she knew not what to feel… But then she met Miss Lucy Steele
Who said that Edward was *her* beau! Poor Elinor, astounded,
Heard worse: they were engaged – a pair! And Edward's ring held *Lucy's* hair…
All hope was gone! She told no-one, though utterly confounded.

The Dashwood sisters went to stay in London; nearly every day
Poor Marianne wrote to her man, but never had an answer.
Then when she met him at a ball, he hardly spoke to her at all
And later wrote a cruel note which proved he was a chancer:

He was to marry someone rich, and so, of course, he'd had to ditch
His Marianne. Dear Colonel Brandon called, all consternation.
The tale he told, though, had them floored – the cad had once seduced his ward!
Their Willoughby, 'twas plain to see, was mired in dissipation.

Now Mrs Ferrars blew a fuse when finally she heard the news
Of Edward's deal with pert Miss Steele. Rejected by his mother,
The son was helped by Colonel B, who offered him a curacy…
Lucy then knew what she must do – hook Robert, Edward's brother!

Meanwhile our girls were on their way to Barton, with a few days' stay
In Somerset. The grass was wet but Marianne, unheeding,
Took lots of walks and caught a chill, which made her soon so very ill
That those who nursed her feared the worst; her life was fast receding.

~Miss Lucy~
~ er! ~
Mrs Ferrars
J.C.F.N

So Brandon, who had not strayed far, rode off to fetch her dear mama.
Then Willoughby incredibly turned up: he'd been mistaken;
He'd been a fool, but now he meant to make confession and repent…
When all was said, he turned and fled, with Elinor left shaken.

Well, Marianne, of course, survived and finally they all arrived
Back home again – and that was when they heard that Mr Ferrars
And Lucy Steele had lately wed; poor Elinor was filled with dread.
When Edward then called round again, she faced the worst of terrors.

At first great agitation reigned but everything was soon explained:
Robert was hitched and *he* was ditched! At last he was unfettered.
He spoke those words which changed her life and thus secured the perfect wife;
As you can guess, their happiness could simply not be bettered.

Then Marianne came down to earth. She understood her sister's worth
And vowed she'd try to modify her reckless wild abandon.
She did! And then a deep love grew for one who'd stayed forever true;
Whate'er the test, he'd loved her best…
Despite his warming flannel vest
She married Colonel Brandon.

Not... Northanger Abbey?

Mrs Ra
UDOLPHO
a Gothic Tale
UDOLPHO
or The veil
Mrs Radcliffe

Miss Catherine Morland as a child was unaccomplished, plain and wild;
A country lass, low middle class, she hated all things formal.
Her teenage years improved her looks; she read – but only *story* books;
Though never very clever, she grew up to be quite normal.

A Mr Allen and his wife, who felt she should see more of life,
Invited Catherine down to Bath for leisure and society;
And there it was that, by and by, one Henry Tilney caught her eye:
A handsome beau and, as men go, a model of propriety.

Then Mrs Allen found a chum in Mrs Thorpe, indulgent mum
Of John, a crass bombastic ass who, though a silly fella,
Was friends with Catherine's brother James (do take good note of all these names!)
James, for his part, had touched the heart of John's sis, Isabella.

When Mr Tilney failed to show, Miss Morland and Miss Thorpe would go
And talk of books and young men's looks and all the latest fashions;
'Udolpho' was their favourite tale (dark goings on behind a veil!)
A scary read, they did concede, which stirred their deepest passions.

But Tilney now filled Catherine's thoughts; his absence put her out of sorts.
Renewed delight came at the sight of Henry's reappearance.
John Thorpe, though, playing Mr Big while driving Catherine in his gig,
Did not impress! You may well guess, she loathed his interference.

Misunderstandings at a dance might well have spoiled this new romance
But Catherine sought and found support from Henry's darling sister.
A second ball brought more success: the couple danced and talked and, yes,
He loved her smile and lack of guile; no Tilney could resist her.

Thorpe intervened, most underhand, to sabotage a walk they'd planned:
A snub perceived; the Tilneys peeved; poor Catherine felt rejected.
But when the rotter tried again, she'd got the measure of him then:
The Tilneys braved; her honour saved; Miss Morland was accepted.

To Catherine, still not worldly wise, came wondrous news: to her surprise
Her nearest and her dearest, James and Bella, were to wed.
The finance that this union brought was maybe less than Bella thought,
Yet, come what may, they'd be OK, or so the lady said.

£5
FIVE
£5
FIVE
£5
FIVE
FIVE
£5
FIVE
J.C.F.

But when her lover was not there – Shock! Horror! – Bella looked elsewhere!
Catherine was hurt to see her flirt with Frederick, Henry's brother.
Then Bella countered with this blow: that *she*'d encouraged *John* (not so!)
Right from the start he'd lost his heart and now he'd have no other.

Certain of Catherine for himself, Thorpe proudly boasted of her wealth;
This news was music to the ears of Henry's greedy pater.
Miss Morland seemed a worthy catch, so General Tilney planned a match:
A rather sad mistake to make, as he would find out later.

Northanger Abbey was his pile and here the Tilneys lived in style.
Back home they went, all most content: Miss Morland was invited.
Strange notions, though, filled Catherine's head, all based, of course, on stuff she'd read:
Might terror loom in some dark room? She really was excited.

At first it seemed she'd got it right: a mystery chest, a stormy night,
A gloomy grove in which to rove, strange rooms that were forbidden,
A death still unexplained, though old, the general heartless, cruel, cold,
A crime she might expose in time, a murder still well hidden...?

LAUNDRY
LIST
THANK YOU
FOR
VISITING

As time went by such fancies fled and pleasures filled the hours instead,
And General T turned out to be attentive, if unbending.
A trip to Henry's own domain did so much more than entertain:
Did Catherine dare to hope that there she'd find her happy ending?

She must, though, give her heart with care, her brother wrote in some despair;
He'd been betrayed: Bella had strayed and nothing would have stopped her.
But all her scheming came to nought for Frederick treated girls as sport,
Added to which she wasn't rich – and so he simply dropped her.

John Thorpe, meanwhile, was in a tizz: Catherine would clearly *not* be his.
He spread the word that he'd now heard Miss Morland had no money.
The general, never prone to doubt, believed him – and threw Catherine out!
Sent home alone, the cause unknown, she didn't find it funny.

When Henry knew, he felt the shame inflicted on the Tilney name
And gave swift chase to Catherine's place to seek her hand in wedlock.
The Morlands, though, would not permit their union with his family split;
Poor Catherine wept and hardly slept, but sadly it was deadlock.

But then a *Viscount* wed Miss T! The general's new-found bonhomie
Made him relent and give consent. His cruel eccentricity
Was now forgiven, in the past, and Henry wed his bride at last;
Thus filial disobedience won true marital felicity.

Or…
was it tyranny at length that gave this marriage extra strength?
We'll never know. Poor Bella, though, faced only harsh rejection.
She'd lost the one who'd really cared; trust broken could not be repaired –
A fitting prize for telling lies and trifling with affection.

Potted Persuasion

BILLS
INVOICE
TO BE
BILL
FINAL DEMAND
PAY NOW
WE VALUE YOUR CUSTOM
Please pay now - PLEASE
VALUED CUSTOMER LETTERS
OVERDUE
THE BARONETAGE
ELLIOT of KELLYNCH
Sir Walter
daughters
Elizabeth
Anne
Mary
heir presumptive
William Elliot
ESTEEMED Sir - your credit limit has

Sir Walter Elliot was vain, a spendthrift no-one could restrain.
The fool at last was told that drastic measures must be taken:
His home at Kellynch must be let – and though he scorned the Navy set,
An admirable admiral moved in and saved his bacon.

Sir Walter went to Bath to stay, with daughter E and Mrs Clay;
She was preferred ('twas quite absurd!) to second daughter Anne.
Anne was a dear, but on the shelf – a shadow of her former self;
Now pale and wan, her bloom had gone since she had lost her man.

A Captain Frederick Wentworth, he, who'd loved her well and tenderly;
Eight years ago this perfect beau by Anne had been rejected
On Lady Russell's 'good' advice. Poor girl, she'd paid a heavy price;
She loved him still – it made her ill – but no-one else suspected.

None then could be more shocked than she when Wentworth was revealed to be
The brother of none other than the admiral's dear wife!
Anne left her home all at a loss, to stay in nearby Uppercross;
The fear that *he* might soon be near just cut her like a knife.

At Uppercross the Musgrove clan was more than pleased to welcome Anne;
Her sister M had missed her, for her kindness never faltered.
And then it happened: Wentworth called! Was he embarrassed? shocked? appalled?
Anne felt estranged; though *he*'d not changed, he found *her* sadly altered.

The Musgrove girls were simply thrilled. Louisa dreamt of hopes fulfilled…
No better, Henrietta felt that *she* must be the one;
Though cousin Hayter pressed his suit, he really was no substitute…
Which of the two would Frederick woo? He wasn't letting on!

Now Captain Wentworth at that time had friends called Harville down in Lyme;
The whole crowd went – quite an event! The Musgroves were ecstatic
Until Louisa, silly clown, from high up on the Cobb jumped down
And hit the deck, a lifeless wreck – so dreadfully dramatic!

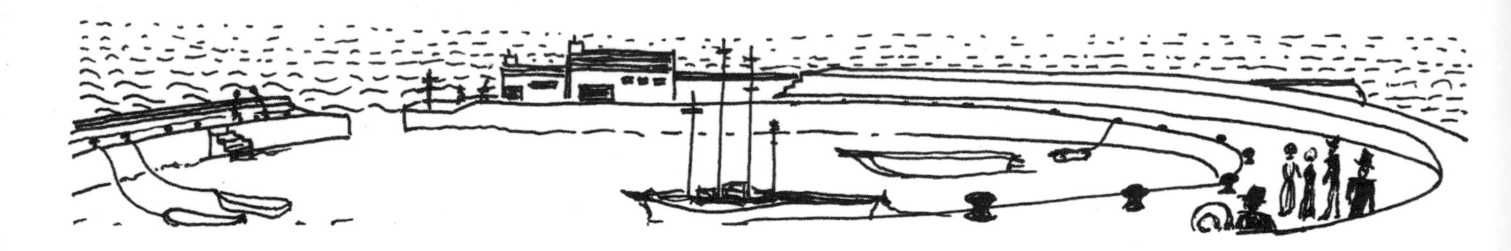

Though badly hurt, she wasn't dead. Anne Elliot kept the coolest head:
She took control – and Wentworth's soul was stirred with deepest feeling.
He stayed at poor Louisa's side, and all assumed *she*'d be his bride,
But in his heart she played no part, sweet Anne the more appealing.

True love, though, knows no easy path, and Anne now disappeared to Bath;
Convivial but trivial, she found its ways alarming.
Young *William* Elliot was there, Anne's cousin and Sir Walter's heir:
Once much despised, he now surprised by being rather charming.

For Lady Russell this was great: she saw in him the ideal mate
For dearest Anne. Then (quel chagrin!) his rival came to visit.
To Lady Russell's great dismay they saw him every other day…
It gave Anne scope once more to hope – a feeling quite exquisite.

Yet more there was to fill her head: Louisa Musgrove was to wed!
At last the die was cast, and what had happened was a marvel:
Dear Wentworth was unshackled, free! For no, indeed, it was not he –
Relief beyond belief! It was a friend of Captain Harville.

A concert was the next affair; Anne's dearest would, of course, be there…
They spoke, they smiled, her heart went wild, and nothing else now mattered.
But seeing her with cousin Will, poor Wentworth left; he'd had his fill.
He could not hide the hurt inside; his dreams, he thought, were shattered.

Now Mrs Smith, a friend in Bath, was fearful of the aftermath
If Will won Anne, as was his plan. (He'd jolly nearly got her!)
She listed those whom he'd misused, and Anne at last was disabused:
She saw her coz for what he was – a calculating rotter.

Harville then called via Uppercross. He spoke to Anne of love and loss,
She told of pain and love in vain, of pure and deep devotion.
Their conversation's every word, by Captain Wentworth overheard,
Smote every part of his poor heart and filled him with emotion.

He seized his pen, he scrawled a note, hardly aware of what he wrote;
It all poured out and left no doubt of what that heart was feeling.
His passion shone through every line, its reassurance was divine…
Could any bliss be sweet as this? It left Anne's senses reeling.

J.C.F.

Such happiness brooks no delay and soon came Frederick's wedding day.
Anne's father rather liked the chap and blessed the glad occasion.
And Lady Russell melted too! She saw the husband's worth and knew
That all along she'd been quite wrong – without too much persuasion.

What happened to our other friends? Jane Austen ties up all the ends:
She let her Henrietta settle down with cousin Hayter,
While William, to great dismay, went off to live with Mrs Clay:
Beyond the pale! But that's a tale that has to wait till … later.

Priceless Park

The daughters of Mr Ward of Huntingdon
J.C.F.

In days of yore Miss Austen told of Fanny Price who, far from bold,
Was sent awhile to uncle's pile, a far-off destination.
Said Thomas Bertram, baronet, "Although this niece we've never met,
We'll take the lass and see she has a decent education."

As Fanny grew to womanhood she worked to serve the common good.
She talked and read with cousin Ed, despite his siblings three
(Maria, Tom and Julia) all finding her peculiar,
While horrid old Aunt Norris made her wretched as could be.

Maria had a suitor who was very rich but stupid too.
Sir Thomas hadn't met him yet – he'd gone off to Antigua.
When folks called Crawford moved nearby from London, one caught Edmund's eye;
Unwary, he let Mary C then find him rather eager.

In every sphere her talents shone; Miss Price paled in comparison.
When on a date to the estate of dear Maria's beau,
Miss Crawford was severely pained to learn that Ed would be ordained;
He found her shame no cause for blame – delusion made it so.

Her brother Henry for his part had captured little Julia's heart
And lit a fire in dear Maria – a shameful, low contrivance!
In theatrical rehearsal then came Julia's reversal when
Maria stole her chosen role, with Henry's full connivance.

They'd hatched a plan to act a play while Fanny's uncle was away;
Ed said "It's wrong!" but could not long resist Miss C's entreaties.
Fanny alone they could not move – she knew the man would disapprove:
In short, she thought that loyalty the duty of a niece is.

Then suddenly Sir Tom was back, the plan was foiled, the gloom was black.
Henry, bereft, just upped and left for Bath, which he found cheerier.
Maria in a fit of pique was wed, not quite within the week
But pretty soon, to that buffoon whom all deemed her inferior.

On his return the Crawford cad conceived of something awful bad:
To add some spice he'd woo Miss Price – he couldn't be rejected.
He saw this wheeze as quite inspired, but then his little scheme backfired
And Henry fell 'neath Fanny's spell, which he had *not* expected!

Haha! Fanny?!!!
OOps!
Maria ✓
Julia ✓
now who?

A second Price we now must meet: a young man sailing with the fleet.
Our Fanny still missed brother Will, far off on some great ocean...
Re-enter Henry with panache! To London town he makes a dash
To plead Will's cause behind closed doors and win his swift promotion.

The bounder thought he'd done enough to win her love, so her rebuff
Hit him quite hard; polite regard was all Miss Price could muster.
Her uncle pressed and so did Ed – can you believe, the dunderhead!
He knew her worth, so why on earth...? It totally nonplussed her.

Sir Thomas, feeling rather bad, packed Fanny off to Mum and Dad
Where squalor, noise and rowdy boys soon drove her to distraction.
She very nearly died of shame when of a sudden Henry came
To press his suit – but, though astute, he got no satisfaction.

From then for weeks her life was dark, though letters came from Mansfield Park:
Ed told of pain and love in vain – so hard for her to handle;
Aunt Bertram sent her tales of woe, for Tom was ill and very low;
Then Mary wrote a cryptic note, forewarning of a scandal.

Yes, soon the fat was in the fire: Henry had run off with Maria!
Elopement with that dope meant she was sure of condemnation.
And Julia, Ed wrote to tell, had hopped it with some ne'er-do-well…
Fanny must come and bring them some much needed consolation.

Three months since she'd first gone away, Ed fetched her home within a day.
He languished still. For good or ill he pined for Crawford's sister;
But Mary blew it, making fun of what the wicked pair had done.
He let her go and, do you know, quite soon he hardly missed her.

And Henry and Maria? Well, they parted after months of hell.
Maria, that pariah, had to face just one more curse,
For old Aunt Norris took her in – a horrid mix of kith and kin,
A move which only goes to prove things *can* always get worse!

And now at last Ed learned to smile; he'd found the heart which knew no guile:
Fanny was wise, her soft light eyes aglow with inner laughter...
Though some may think this ending trite, *I* think Jane Austen got it right.
She wed her Ed and, so it's said, lived happy ever after.

SHE WED
HER ED
her TED
her FRED
her HENRY
her GEORGE
her FITZWILLIAM

WHO?!?
?
FITZWILLIAM?

Pruned
&
Prejudiced

Rich, young, handsome
gentlemen are most
WELCOME
to
LONGBOURN

The Netherfield estate was let to Mr Bingley. He as yet
Was unattached; to see him matched with one of her five daughters
Was Mrs Bennet's big idea. Affording her still more good cheer
A regiment of men was sent to nearby army quarters.

The younger girls went down a storm with all the men in uniform;
The eldest, Jane, was soon to gain young Bingley's deep affection,
While Mr Darcy, Bingley's guest, liked sparky Lizzy Bennet best
Though he was vain and felt disdain for such a low connection.

While calling on the Bingleys, Jane got rather wet out in the rain;
She caught a cold and so was told to stay till she was better.
To see her, Lizzy walked for miles through muddy fields and over stiles:
Amazed, appalled and quite enthralled, Darcy could not forget her.

Back home to general dismay their clergy cousin came to stay:
Collins was heir (it wasn't fair!) to all the Bennet acres.
Ingratiatingly absurd, he weighed his every pompous word.
He sought a wife to fill his life, but so far had no takers.

In contrast, on the army's books was Mr Wickham. His good looks
Caught Lizzy's eye, and by and by they met in conversation;
He told how Darcy's wicked ways had cruelly consigned his days
Most shamefully to poverty and great humiliation.

The Bingleys organised a ball, but Wickham didn't show at all.
Lizzy was cross and blamed the loss on Darcy. It was gruesome,
For Mr Collins made her dance (he planned to woo her for the manse!)
When Darcy led her out instead, they made a striking twosome.

But Mr Collins knew his mind; he popped the question – she declined.
His grief and disbelief were brief, in fact he scarcely tarried
But turned to Charlotte, Lizzy's friend, who longed for spinsterhood to end.
Freedom from need thus guaranteed, she let herself be married.

Meanwhile the Bingleys left for town, leaving poor Jane so very down.
Bingley, 'twas said, could soon be wed to Darcy's little sister.
A plot! thought Lizzy, rarely fooled. Her Mr Wickham too had cooled:
He'd met a lass with lots of brass and couldn't quite resist her.

. . . singled you out to be the companion of my future life
It is a right thing for every clergyman . . . to set the example of matrimony within his parish!
When I do myself the honour of speaking to you next on this
I must interrupt him soon . . . No! No! No! NO!
Now nothing remains for me but . . to assure you in most animated language of my affection for you . . .
It will add to MY happiness . . .
. . . the very noble lady whom I have the honour of calling patroness said "Mr. Collins, you must marry . . .
J.C.F.

DESPITE.....
I must ask you to..
MARRY
ME!!
NEVER!
Jane
Dear Lizzy

An invitation Charlotte sent had Lizzy setting off for Kent,
For Hunsford where the Collins pair were tolerably settled.
The parson's patron, Lady C, received her condescendingly:
She was all swank and pulled her rank, but Lizzy wasn't nettled.

Then Darcy came to join the fun! He was this lady's sister's son;
In him she saw a son-in-law before he was much older.
Her daughter, though, was pale and small – not Darcy's cup of tea at all;
For him the prize of sparkling eyes and spirits that were bolder...

So in a gesture fine and grand, he called and asked for Lizzy's hand
Against his will – his feeling still was one of degradation.
He was amazed to be refused, reproved most harshly, then accused:
He got the blame for Wickham's shame and Jane's sad separation.

Feelings on both sides were intense. He wrote to her in his defence:
Wickham had lied; the cad had tried his hand at double-dealing.
The details all fell into place. How blind she'd been in Wickham's case!
How partial too! But now she knew the truth; it left her reeling.

The regiment then went away to Brighton – what a sorry day!
Young Lydia perfidiously got herself invited
To stay there with the colonel's wife, an act which was to change her life.
Her parents, though, just let her go, which Lizzy thought short-sighted.

By now I should have made it clear that Darcy came from Derbyshire.
Lizzy, while staying there, one day was taken out to visit
His splendid Pemberley estate, and there by some strange quirk of fate
The man appeared – just as she'd feared; her terror was exquisite.

But he was changed: he wasn't rude! Kind invitations then ensued.
She went to call and found that all was amity around her.
To interrupt this semi-bliss, bad news arrived; its gist was this:
That giddy little Lydie had absconded with a bounder!

To cut a complex story short, the couple were pursued and caught.
Wickham ('twas he!) was made to see he'd not been very clever.
Poor Lizzy suffered from the blow – Darcy, of course, had had to know;
She feared the shame heaped on her name would put him off for ever.

The more she learned, the worse it got: Darcy, it seemed, had fixed the lot!
He'd gone to town and tracked them down, he'd got the cad promotion,
He'd seen them married (with regret) and paid off Wickham's massive debt...
These marvels were all done for *her* through unalloyed devotion.

Back home there was a shock in store: Bingley and Darcy at the door!
All was delight in Bingley's sight, though Jane was in a tizzy;
But now, with Darcy on their side, Bingley soon won her for his bride:
It had to be. Then Lady C turned up to talk to Lizzy!

Her rantings would have made you blench: Were Darcy and this upstart wench...
Were they *engaged*? She was enraged and wanted this refuted.
Such cheek was not to be endured; she wanted to be reassured
That Pemberley would never be so horribly polluted.

Lizzy refused! And that was when her lover dared to hope again.
He cast aside his former pride and showed that he had heeded
The message of her harsh reproof; he'd changed: no longer proud, aloof...
His heart was true and now she knew his love was all she needed.

The other Bennets were amazed (and Collins was distinctly fazed!)
When she said 'yes'. With great success the couple were united.
At Pemberley they lived in style and all but Lady C could smile...
And thus, dear friends, the story ends – with all of us delighted.

REGISTER OF MARRIAGES
Reverend P. ELTON ≈ Augusta HAWKINS
Frank Weston CHURCHILL ≈ Jane FAIRFAX
Robert MARTIN Fmr. ≈ Harriet SMITH
George KNIGHTLEY ≈ Emma WOODHOUSE
VISCOUNT Anon. ≈ Eleanor TILNEY
Henry TILNEY ≈ Catherine MORLAND
John WILLOUGHBY ≈ Sophia GREY
Robert FERRARS ≈ Lucy STEELE
Edward FERRARS ≈ Elinor DASHWOOD
Colonel BRANDON ≈ Marianne DASHWOOD
REGISTER OF MARRIAGES
Captain J. BENWICK ≈ Louisa MUSGROVE
Charles HAYTER ≈ Henrietta MUSGROVE
Frederick WENTWORTH ≈ Anne ELLIOT
Mr RUSHWORTH ≈ Maria BERTRAM
John YATES ≈ Julia BERTRAM
Edmund BERTRAM ≈ Fanny PRICE
William COLLINS ≈ Charlotte LUCAS
George WICKHAM ≈ Lydia BENNET
Charles BINGLEY ≈ Jane BENNET
Fitzwilliam DARCY ≈ Elizabeth BENNET
J.C.F.

Fitzwilliam?
~ DARCY ~
Of course !!

Margaret Dews has been writing in rhyme for as long as she can remember and has loved these novels since schooldays in Dudley. A member of the Northern Branch of the Jane Austen Society since its inception, she now lives in Stratford-upon-Avon, but has no plans to tackle the Bard!

Christine Fitton lives in Nottinghamshire where she is an active member of both the Retford and Rufford Art Societies. This is the first time she has produced a collection of book illustrations. She has enjoyed herself enormously in the process, especially re-reading all the novels yet again.

The Jane Austen Society aims to foster the appreciation and study of Jane Austen's life and work, to secure the preservation of her manuscripts, letters and other memorabilia, and to support the work of the Jane Austen Memorial Trust in maintaining the museum at the novelist's house in Chawton, Hampshire.

The Northern Branch was established in 1999 and now has over 160 members. It has a most active patron in Irene Collins, author of *Jane Austen and the Clergy* and *Jane Austen: The Parson's Daughter*. Regular events include lectures, study days, informal discussions and summer outings. Its tri-annual magazine, *Impressions,* is a lively mix of erudite and light-hearted contributions from members.

For further information on the Jane Austen Society and its associated Branches and Groups, see **www.janeaustensociety.org.uk**